EXCEL 2025

---

0 TO EXPERT

THE ULTIMATE CRASH COURSE PRACTICAL STEP-BY-STEP GUIDE ON HOW TO MASTER EXCEL IN LESS 72 HOURS.

PAUL CASTLE

INDEX

INTRODUCTION

Excel does much more than most people imagine: as a spreadsheet, Excel efficiently processes large amounts of data and offers exceptional tools for communicating results. For those with intermediate or advanced skills, a spreadsheet can do much more: for example, it can become a tool for tracking activities or an analysis tool to help make decisions. For those who are also well versed in automation, Excel can be transformed into more or less complex management or advanced processing tools such as configurators or planners and so on.

With Excel, we can do everything or nothing, depending on the cono- scence we have: with a basic knowledge of Excel, we can share work and results, check, regi- rate, and process data, perform data analysis, create struc-

ments, reports, summary tables and charts. But, to do all this, you need to know Excel well enough to use it effectively and efficiently. This usually requires one or more courses, dozens of hours of learn- ing, and hundreds of hours of practice.Fortunately, having purchased this manual will save you time and help you learn the basics. One of the skills most underestimated by Excel users is knowledge of interaction tools: I am referring to the spreadsheet interface, that is, a set of ready-made tools that offer controls to execute various commands, open dialog boxes, and . Excel offers hundreds of buttons, icons, windows, settings, etc., and of this multitude few are unnecessary or redundant, and each control has a specific function and purpose. Our goal, of course, is to find out where the tool's most useful buttons are located and how they are used. From the outset, we need to spend time learning how to use the ribbon, which gives us access to 90 percent of Excel's tools.We will not use it all the time, but it is important to know it thoroughly. Only when we have become true Excel experts will we use the keyboard sequences, object controls, such as Excel charts and tables, and the conte- stual menu, the one that is invoked by right-clicking. We will discover all this step by step as this manual will enable us to have and acquire a complete cono- scence of Excel; the program is divided as follows. Chapters 1 through 3 cover the basics for any Excel user, the fundamentals and learning Excel, starting with

there

from the interface, basic and intermediate functions, and data analysis. Chapter 4 covers data visualization and delve into advanced graphs and dashboards for professio- nal management of visual information. Chapters 5, 6, and 7 focus on advanced analysis, data modeling, and managing large data sets, starting with basic concepts and delving into the use of Power Pivot, Power Query, and other professional techniques. Chapter 8 covers automation and design with Excel. Chapters 9 to 15 will discuss integration issues with other tools and advanced features such as integration with Python, ERP, Power Automate even Excel customization, followed by key aspects such as data validation, debugging, and VBA code optimization. Finally, Chapter 16 covers final optimiz- ation with a focus on VBA, which is the final step for those who want to specialize in process au- tomation and advanced data management in Excel. Let's turn on our pc, open Excel, and we're ready to get started.

I REMIND YOU THAT AT THE END OF THE BOOK THERE WILL BE 2 PRICELESS BONUSES TO REDEEM:

- AN ENTIRE COURSE ON HOW TO LEARN EXCEL FROM 0 WITH OVER 12 HOURS.

- WHATS APP CHANNEL DEDICATED TO EXCEL AND ON VARIOUS COMPUTER TOPICS

1

EXCEL BASICS

The Excel interface

The first thing to do when opening Excel is to familiarize yourself with its interface. This consists of several main sections.

We have the menu bar, which is located at the top, and contains the tabs of *File*, *Home, Insert*, *Page Layout*. Each of these tabs then, encloses specific commands. Next we find the formula bar, which is below the multifunction bar that we will now look at.This bar shows the contents of the cell that we are going to select, and it is here that we can enter text, values or formulas. When we select a tab, a bar will appear with icons representing the main functions: this is the multifunction bar. For example, the *Home* tab includes.

options to format text, apply borders and nume- ry formats. The main space, on the other hand, organized into nume- rate rows and columns indicated by the letters of the alphabet where the intersection between a row and a column is the cell, is the worksheet. Finally, at the bottom, we find the sheet tabs that allow us to switch from one worksheet to another within the same workbook, or the same file.

Practical exercise:

To understand how the program works, let's try opening Excel and observe its interface: click on the various menu tabs to explore its functions and then try selecting any cell and observe how the contents of the formula bar changes.

Data entry and management

Cells are the heart of Excel, and each cell can contain a number, a date, text or formulas. To add content to a cell, then to enter data, click-call on the desired cell and type in the value, then press Enter. If we double-click on a cell, we can edit a data item, thus its contents, or select it and use the formula bar. If, on the other hand, we want to select a single cell, a range, or an entire row or column, we simply click on the row or column header.

Practical exercise:

We enter in cell A1 the value "Sales" and then in cell A2 the value "100"; we copy the contents of A2 to cell B2 using the Copy (Ctrl+C) and Paste (Ctrl+V) functions.

Basic formatting

Excel offers numerous formatting tools accessible from the *Home* tab.Formatting is one of its main, perhaps essential, tools because it allows us to make data more organized and readable.

To create tables that are visually neater, we can use borders that can be applied to either a single cell, a range of cells or the entire sheet. With basic formatting we can also change font type, color, size or alignment of text within one or more cells. Another type of formatting concerns numeric formats and their display. For example, we can to see numbers as they are we use the *General* command; the *Currency* command will show us numbers with a monetary symbol, for example in €, and finally the *Percentage* command allows us to convert a number to a percentage, for example 0.50 becomes 50%.

Practical exercise:

We write in cell A1 "Turnover" and apply the gras- sect; then we go on to enter in cell B1 the value "1500" and format the cell as "Currency" using the Home tab. Finally, we apply a border to the box that includes cells A1 to B1.

Creating a simple graph

Thanks to Excel, we can very quickly and easily create different types of graphs that allow us to display data in a clear and appealing way. To do this we simply select the data and go to the *Insert* tab, then choose the type of graph, such as pie, bar or line graph. Once the chart is created we can move on to customizing it by choosing and editing fonts, titles, layouts and colors.

Practical exercise:

We enter in column A the data A1: "Product A," A2: "Product B," A3: "Product C." In column B, we enter the quantities sold: B1: "50", B2: "30", B3: "20". Finally, select interval A1, go to Insert> bar graph

Filters and sorting

When we have to work with large amounts of data, we can rely on two tools to succeed in our task: filters and sorting. The former, allow us to display only data that meet certain criteria; with sorting, on the other hand, we can reorder data alphabetically or numerically.

Practical exercise:

We create a list of names (column A) and their ages (column B); we select the data, going to Data > Sort and sorting the names alphabetically, then apply a filter to show only people older than 30.

Basic formulas

Formulas are the backbone of Excel and allow us to perform automatic calculations. Any formula always begins with the symbol =. For example, if we want to sum two numbers in cells A1 and A2, we will go and write =A1+A2 in cell A3. Excel offers predefined functions, such as SUM, AVERAGE and MIN, that simplify calculations. If, for example, we want to calculate an average, we use: =MAX(A1:A10); if instead we want to sum a range of cells, we will use: =SUM(A1:A10).

Practical exercise:

Let's enter the numbers "5," "10" and "15" in cells A1, A2 and A3 respectively; in cell A4, let's enter the formula =SUM(A1:A3) and press Enter. Let us now try changing one of the values, for example, the value 15 becomes 20, and we can observe how the result in cell A4 will automatically update.

2

FORMULAS AND INTERMEDIATE FUNCTIONS

We will now explore the advanced tools offered by Excel, which include a variety of formulas and intermediate-level functions. These tools are essential for automating complex calculations, manipulating text strings with precision, managing dates and times efficiently, and taking advantage of logical search and reference functions. These capabilities are foundational for those who wish to elevate their skills in advanced data a- nalysis and management through this powerful spreadsheet software.

Logic functions

Logic functions allow us to perform condition-based operations and are found to be essential for self-matizing decisions and calculations.

IF

The SE function returns a different result depending on whether a condition is true or false.

Parameter configuration:

```
=SE(test_logico; valore_se_vero; valore_se_falso)
```

Let's take an example: if there is a value in cell A1 that corresponds to 100, and we want to check whether it is greater than 50 and return "Passed" or "Not Passed," we need to enter: =SE(A1>50; "Passed"; "Not passed").

Practical exercise:

We enter in cell A1 the value "100" and in cell B1 we inse- rate: =SE(A1>=50; "Promoted"; "Failed"). We then go to change the value in A1 and could see how the result changes in B1.

E and O

These two functions are used in combination with SE to check multiple conditions. The E function returns TRUE only if all the conditions are true; while the O function remains TRUE if at least one condition is true. For example:

=SE(E(A1>50; B1>50); "Both above 50"; "At least one below 50");

=SE(O(A1>50; B1>50); "At least one above 50"; "Both below 50").

Practical exercise:

We enter two numbers in cells A1 and B1, then write in cell C1: =SE(E(A1>10; B1>10); "Both valid"; "Invalid"). Now we change the values and check the result.

Search and reference functions

Search functions, allow you to extract data from large tables or datasets and the most important are: SEARCH.VERT, SEARCH.ORIZZ, INDEX and COMPARE.

SEARCH.VERT (Vertical Search)

This function is used to look up a value in a column and return a corresponding value.

Parameter configuration:

```
=CERCA.VERT(valore; tabella; indice_colonna;
[intervallo])
```

The value is the item to be searched, the **table** the range in which to search, the **column_index** is the number of the column containing the value to be returned, and finally, the **range** is FALSE for an exact match, TRUE for an approximate one. For example, if we have a table with product IDs in column A and prices in column B, we can find the price of the product with ID "101" using:

```
=CERCA.VERT(101; A1:B10; 2; FALSO)
```

Practical exercise:

We enter the data into a table: A1: "ID"; B1: "Price"; A2: "101"; B2: "50"; A3: "102"; B3: "70." Now we write in cell C1: =CERCA.VERT(102; A2:B3; 2; FALSE).

INDEX and COMPARISON

The two functions provide us with an alternative to Vertical Search: **INDEX** returns the value of a specific cell in a range, and instead **COMPARE** finds the position of a value in a range.

Parameter configuration:

```
INDICE(intervallo; riga; [colonna])
CONFRONTA(valore; intervallo; [tipo_correlazione])
```

Suppose we have a table with: A1: "Product"; B1: "Price"; A2: "Apple"; B2: "2" and A3: "Banana"; B3: "1.5." In order to find the price of "Banana," we will use: =CONFRONT("Banana"; A2:A3; 0) returns 2 (the row of "Banana") and =INDICE(B2:B3; 2) returns 1.5.

Practical exercise:

Using the Product, Price, Apple and Banana data just written, let's enter them into an Excel sheet: we use COMPARE to find the "Banana" row, while INDEX to get the corresponding price.

Text functions

With the text functions, which are CONCATENA, RIGHT, LEFT, and LENGTH, Excel allows us to manipulate text strings.

CONCATENA (or CONCAT)

Combines two or more strings into one.

Parameter configuration:

```
=CONCATENA(testo1; testo2; ...)
```

For example, if A1 contains "First Name" and B1 contains "Last Name," we will use: =CONCATENA(A1; " "; B1) to get "First Name Last Name."

RIGHT, LEFT, STRING.EXTRACT

These three functions allow us to extract portions of the text: with **RIGHT(text; num_characters)**, we will be returned the last characters, with **LEFT(text; num_characters)** the first ones, and with **STRINGA.EXTRACT(text; start; num_characters)** a portion of the text from a specific position.

For example, if we want the value 45 to be returned, we would write:

=DESTRA("12345"; 2); for the value 123 we will write: =LEFT("12345"; 3); and finally for the BCD value write- remo: =STRINGA.EXTRACT("ABCDE"; 2; 3).

Practical exercise:

We write a simple sentence in cell A1, such as, "Excel is great" in cell A1: if we use LEFT we might extract the first 5 characters; using RIGHT, we will extract the last 9.

Date and time functions

If we need to have to work on time calculations, we will have to use the functions related to date and time.

TODAY and NOW

TODAY(): returns us the current date; NOW(): returns us the current date and time.

For example, taking any date (in this case 22/11/2024) as an object, with the function =DATE() we will have "2024-11-22"; with the function =ADDATE() we will have date and time, thus: "2024-11-22 09:08".

DATA.DIFF.

This is the function that allows us to be able to calculate the diffe- rence between two dates.

Parameter configuration:

```
=DATA.DIFF(data_inizio; data_fine; unità)
```

The unit may be: "Y": then the difference in years; "M": the difference in months; and "D," the difference in days.

For example, if we want to calculate the age of a person who was born on February 13, 1990, we will have to enter the following function: =DATA.DIFF(DATE(1990;13;2); TODAY(); "Y").

3

DATA ANALYSIS IN EXCEL

With Excel we have the possibility of analyzing a large amount of data: thanks to its features, we can inter- pret, explore and organize different information, always in a perfect way. Data analysis is essentially based on creation and use tables, filters, graphs, and statistical collection and organization features.

Advanced tables and filters

By creating tables, with Excel we can recreate an organized structure that allows us to manage and analyze data by applying filters, dynamic formatting and formulas. Tables allow us to easily manage filters and sorting, you can customize them to your need or liking, and you can also automatically update formulas whenever new data is entered.

To create a table we will simply select the data range, including the column headers, move to the *Insert* tab and click on *Table*, then confirm the range and make sure the *Table with Headers* option is selected.

With advanced filters, we are able to isolate specific data simply based on complex conditions. To appli- cate them, we need only go to the *Data* tab and select *Advanced Filter*; then we must specify a criteria range that includes the filter conditions in a sepa- rate table; and finally choose between *Filter the list in place* or *Copy to another range*.

Let's take an example:

Suppose we have a table with sales and we want to filter rows where sales exceed 500. We then go on to create a criteria table with a corresponding header, "Sales" > 500, then apply the advanced filter using this table as the criteria.

Pivot tables

Another essential and powerful tool in Excel is pivot tables, which are useful for visualizing, summarizing and analyzing data. To create a pivot table we will first go to select the data we want to analyze: then we go to the *Insert* tab and click on *Pivot Table*; we then choose whether to inse- rve the table in a new sheet or an existing one; we move to the *Pivot Table Fields* window and drag and drop the fields into the "columns" areas, if we want to create column headings; "filters" if we want to apply global filters; "rows" to subdivide the data into rows; and into "values" if we need to calculate averages, counts or simply to sum the data.

If we need to do more advanced analysis, in a pivot table we can also add calco- lated fields: for example, if we want to calculate profit by having cost and sales data, we can go to the *Analyze* tab, click on *Fields, Elements and Set> Calculated Field*, then enter the formula: =Sales-Cost.

Practical example:

We have a table that has the columns Product, Region, Sales; let's go and drag Product to the Rows area, Region to the Columns area, and Sales to the Values area: by doing this we can get a table showing sales by product in each region.

Statistical analysis with functions

If we find ourselves in the position of needing to analyze data, we can do so with Excel using statistical analysis functions. The most common statistical functions are:

- **CORRELATION**: which evaluates the relationship between two variables =CORRELATION(A1:A10; B1:B10)
- **DEV.ST**: which calculates the standard deviation for a sample =DEV.ST(A1:A10)
- **AVERAGE**: which calculates the arithmetic mean =MEDIA(A1:A10)
- **MEDIAN**: which returns the central value of an interval =MEDIAN(A1:A10)
- **MODA.SNGL**: which returns the most frequent value in a range =MODA.SNGL(A1:A10)

But Excel's *Data* tab also includes advanced tools for analysis: in fact, here if we click on *Data Analysis* we can find features such as: analysis of variance (ANOVA), linear regression and descriptive statistics.

Practical example:

Suppose we have in column A data on advertising and in column B data on sales. We go to the Data Analysis menu and select Regression; now we set the variable Sales, then the dependent variable, and the variable

Advertisement, the independent one: in this way, we will able to obtain a report with coefficient of determination (R^2) and p-value.

Advanced graphs

If we want to represent data visually for immediate interpretations, we will use advanced graphs: pivot graphs, Sparkline graphs, and combination graphs.

Pivot charts are based on pivot table data and update automatically when the underlying data changes. To create a pivot chart we need only, after creating the pivot table, move to the *Insert* tab and click on *Pivot* Chart: here we need only choose a chart type (e.g., bar or pie).

Sparkline graphs are smaller graphs that are inserted into a single cell for the purpose of showing trends. To create them we move to the *Insert* tab and click on *Sparkline*: then choose a data range and specify where to insert the graph.

Combined graphs, finally, are those graphs that allow us to display two sets of data with different scales: for example, if we want to compare sales and revenue margins, we can select the data, going to *Insert > Combined Graph*; then we assign a different type of graph to each series, such as a line for margins and columns for sales.

What-If Analysis

If we find ourselves needing to hypothesize scenarios and forecasts, for example of sales, future, how do we do it? Excel provides us with *What-If* analysis: we will see into the future simply by changing input values.

The first step is to do a goal search, that is, to find the value needed to reach an X result: let's say we want to know in advance how much merchandise we will have to sell in order to reach a profit of €25,000: we then go to *Data > Analysis Tools > Goal Search* and then specify the cell we want to change (so the cell of units sold) and then the goal we want to reach, the €25,000.

The second step involves the data tables, which show us how the results will be able to change as one or more variables change: for example, let's go and create a formula for calculating profit, thus: =Sales-Cost; let's use the data table to vary sales prices and observe the impact on profit.

The last step concerns, precisely, the scenarios that may lie ahead. We can create a simple future scenario-

mind by going to *Data* > *Analysis Tools* > *Scenario Management* and creating scenarios such as "Optimistic," "Pessimistic," and "Realistic": finally, we only need to enter the values for each scenario and analyze the results obtained, which may or may not be in line with our prediction.

4

ADVANCED DATA VISUALIZATION

In order to be able to present our data in a clear and understandable way, detect trends, check for anomalies, or put in writing the insights from a job, which diffi- cultly would be easy to handle in a regular sheet, Excel helps us with data visualization. This compo- nent can range from simple visualization to combined graphs to interactive dashboards that can create truly functional presentations.

Combined and advanced graphs

A combination graph allows us to display two different types of data, such as categorical data and numerical data, within the same graph, using different types of graphs. This tool is useful if we want to compare data with some different scales, such as when we need to use a histo- gram for absolute values and a line for a moving average. To create a combined graph we need to select our data range, then go to the *Insert* tab and choose *Combined Graph*: we need to choose the type of graph for each data set, such as a column graph for sales and a line graph for profit margin. Finally, we can also customize the secondary axis by right-clicking on one of the data sets and selecting *Add Secondary Axis*.

Practical example:

Suppose we have two sets of data, on the one hand the monthly sales of a product expressed in quantity, and on the other hand the monthly advertising expenditure expressed in euros; using a combined graph with histograms for sales and a line for advertising expenditure, we will be able to clearly visualize the relationship between these two variables.

Scatter plot: the Scatter

In scatter plots each point on the graph represents a pair of values; we can use them if we need to show the relationship between two numerical variables, when we want to visua- lize trends, whether linear or nonlinear, or when we want to identify outliers or anomalies in the data. To create a scatter plot we need to select the data, i.e., two columns of numbers, then go to *Insert > Scatter Plot* and choose the type of plot; finally, we can customize the axes, points, and titles to better clarify the relationship between the variables.

Interactive dashboards in Excel

A dashboard is a set of charts, pivot tables, indicators, then a set of visualizations that allows us to quickly monitor and analyze business performance or other indicators. With Excel, we can create interat- tive dashboards that allow users to interact with data to view different information as needed. To create a basic dashboard we first import the data we want to visualize using either a pivot table or Power Pivot; then we link the data to the pivot tables and then go on to add interactive controls: we use the visual filter (slicer) and scrollbars, so we can select different data ranges or time periods; to add a slicer to a pivot table we go to *Insert > Slicer;*, we go to *Developer > Controls > Scrollbar* instead.

If, on the other hand, we want to use Power Pivot, which allows us to handle large volumes of data and create complex models for our dashboards, we need only import data from different sources and

Create a relationship between tables. To do this, we first enable Power Pivot using this shortcut: *File > Options > Add-ons > Power Pivot*. Then we create a Pivot table by linking several tables via relationships and finally add DAX formulas to calculate advanced metrics such as profit margins or growth trends.

Practical example: imagine we want to create a dashboard of sales performance for an entire quarter; we can create a pivot table aggregating sales by month and a column chart showing sales by product. Using a slicer, each user could filter the data by region or by time period.

Graph customization

Excel allows us to fully customize any chart and/or table within a sheet: we can thus change fonts, colors, add labels, change trend lines, and much more. Data labels, can be added if we want to improve the compren- sion of a sheet, to add them we simply go to *Chart Layout > Data Labels*; if, on the other hand, we want to change the type of chart, we click on the chart and simply choose the various options that Excel offers us; if we want to color charts and tables, or change the color of the data to improve their readability or match the colors to the company brand, we go to *Format> Fill Color*. If we want to, then, highlight trends in the data, we will simply add trend lines or moving averages to the graphs: so, we select the graph and go to *Analyze> Add Trend Line* and choose the type whether linear or exponential (again, we can customize the trend line to include the formula or R^2 value). Should we find ourselves working on a time series, we opt for a moving average to help smooth out short-term fluctuations: by adding it to a line graph, we can best visualize long-term trends.

Charts with Excel functions: the Slicer

With Excel, we can create graphs that update auto- matically based on the data entered: the graphs adapt dina- mically to different data selections, creating an interactive experience for the user. The functions that allow us this mode are: IF, INDEX, COMPARISON, and SUM.IF. The latter formula, for example, allows us to filter the data and then link the result to the graph: thus we could create a graph that shows only data above a certain threshold.

Slicers, on the other hand, are one of the most powerful tools for adding interactivity to reports in Excel: in addition to traditional filters, slicers allow us to filter data visually, enhancing the user experience. To create a Slicer, we select a pivot table, go to *Insert > Slicer* and choose the fields from which we want to filter data; then, we use slicers to easily interact with the data and automatically update the charts. We can also add multiple slicers that control different pivot tables simultaneously: to do this, we select a slicer, go to *Options*

> *Connections* and choose the pivot tables to connect.

5

DATA MODELING AND FORECASTING

To analyze large datasets and forecast future trends, we use data modeling and forecasting with Excel: with tools such as Power Pivot, DAX calculations, and the *Analysis Tools* add-on, they provide us with a powerful ecosystem for building complex data models and calculating forecasts.

Power pivot

As mentioned in the previous chapter, Power Pivot is an advanced data modeling tool for analyzing large volumes of data from different sources, ideal for creating relationships between tables, performing complex calculations, and generating detailed reports. First, we need to make sure that Power Pivot is enabled: go to *File> Options> Additional Components,* select

COM add-ons from the drop-down menu and click *Go*; then check *Microsoft Power Pivot for Excel* and press *OK*.

In doing so, we can create a data model: first, we load data into Excel from different sources such as SQL, Access, or CSV files, using this shortcut *Power Pivot > Manage > Add Data.*

Once the data is imported, we go to *Diagram View* to create relationships between tables: then drag and drop related fields between tables to define a relationship e.g., *Customer ID* between an order table and a customer table.

Calculations with DAX

The acronym DAX, which stands for "*Data Analysis Expressions*," identifies a formula language used in Power Pivot that is used to create advanced calculations and custom metrics.

Among the various useful functions of DAX we have:

- ALCULATE: useful for applying custom filters;
- RELATED: if we want to access values from other related tables;
- SUMX: if we need to calculate sums based on specific conditions.

Let's try to create a DAX formula to calculate the profit margin:

```plaintext
Margine di Profitto= SUM(Vendite[Profitto])/SUM(Vendite[Entrate])
```

Sensitivity analysis

To analyze in detail and depth how changes in parameters affect the results of a model or calculation, Excel offers advanced tools such as "data tables" and the "scenario manager." These tools enable sensitivity analysis, i.e., a study aimed at understanding the impact of changes in key variables on the final results, in a simple, effective and well-structured way.

"Data Tables" are ideal for analyzing one or two varia- bles; to create one we must first organize our data with the independent variable in a column or row and the calculated results in the cell; we go to *Data> Analysis of*

Simulation > Data Table, we select the input cell for the independent variable and press *OK*.

The "Scenario Manager" allows us to create and compare different scenarios based on alternative assumptions. To use it we go to *Data > Simulation Analysis > Scenario Manager* and create scenarios by specifying values for key variables such as price, cost and quantity; finally we use the *Summary Report* to compare results.

Practical example: let's try to calculate how profits change based on changes in production costs and sales prices; to do this we use a two-variable Data Table to analyze all combinations.

Forecasts and regression models

Excel includes functionality to build predictive models and generate forecasts based on historical data.

The PREVISION.ETS function is designed to create predictions based on temporal data, and is useful for forecasting sales, demand, or any other metric with temporal trends.

Parameter configuration:

```plaintext
PREVISIONE.ETS(valore_destinato;valori_dati;valori_temporali;[stagion
alità])
```

Practical example:

Suppose we have a time series of monthly sales for three years, and we use FORECAST.ETS to estimate sales for the next six months. We select an empty cell and write:

```plaintext
=PREVISIONE.ETS(A37; B2:B36; A2:A36)
```

In this sequence A37 is the future time value, B2:B36 are the historical data, and A2:A36 are the corresponding periods.

Linear regression, on the other hand, is a statistical method for analyzing the relationship between an independent variable and a dependent variable. To run a regression with Excel, we go to *Data> Analysis Tools> Regression Analysis* and inse- rate *Input Range Y* (thus the data of the dependent variable) and *Input Range X* (the data of the independent variable); finally, we check *Output* to display the results.

Practical example:

We try to analyze the impact of advertising spending on sales. The regression provides the correlation coefficient (R^2), which measures the strength of the relationship, and the equation of the regression line, which can be used for future predictions.

Modeling with Power Query

Another advanced tool for preparing and transforming data in Excel, which allows us to model data before importing it into the worksheet, is Power Query. To load data with Power Query we go to *Data > Get Data > From File,* import our data from CSV, Excel or external database files, and use the Power Query interface to combine tables, filter data and remove columns that are unnecessary for our purpose.

With we can perform custom calculations, thanks to its M language: for example, we can recalculate values by adding a 20% margin:

```plaintext
= Table.AddColumn(#"Dati Importati", "Prezzo con Margine", each
[Prezzo Base] * 1.2)
```

Advanced analysis tools

Target Search calculates the input value needed to obtain a specific result; for example, let's say we want to know how many units we need to sell to reach a profit target of €25,000. We go to *Data > Simulation Analysis > Target Search* and specify the target cell, i.e., profit, the target value, our €25,000, and the variable cell, i.e., quantity. *The Solver*, on the other hand, is a tool for optimizing outcomes, such as maximizing profits or minimizing costs, with specific constraints. Let's say we want to find the optimal combination of products to produce, while respecting resource constraints. We use the *Solver* function to set maximum profit, then an objective function, quantities produced, then decision variables, and resource availability, i.e., constraints.

6

COMPLETE GUIDE TO PIVOT TABLES IN EXCEL

Pivot tables are one of Excel's most powerful tools for analyzing, summarizing, and visualizing large amounts of data. With just a few clicks, you can turn a complex worksheet into a clear, readable report. You will be able to use the advanced features of pivot tables, including creating custom calculations, using advanced filters, and handling time groupings.

Creating a Pivot Table

The first step when we need to create a pivot table is to prepare the data: let's make sure that the data are organized in table format with clear headings and no blank rows. We then highlight the cell range, or use an Excel table, and proceed to insert the pivot table by going to *Insert> Pivot Table* and choose whether to create the table in a new sheet or an existing one. At this point we can build the table by simply dragging and dropping fields into the *Rows, Columns, Values* and *Filters* section to organize the data.

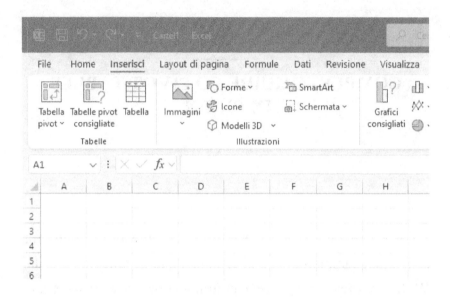

Create advanced custom calculations

Pivot tables can be enhanced with calculated fields and calculated elements to perform complex analyses. A calculated field allows you to add formulas that operate on the pivot table data. Suppose we want to calculate a profit margin based on sales and costs: we click on the pivot table and go to *Pivot Table Tools > Analyze > Fields, Elements and Sets > Calculated Field.* We will now simply enter a formula that will create a field that calculates the profit for each row, namely the following:

```
Excel
=Vendite - Costi
```

Calculated elements, on the other hand, work within an existing field to perform calculations among the elements of that field.

Using advanced filters and time groupings

Filters allow you to restrict the data displayed in a pivot table based on specific criteria. Slicers, for example, are visual tools that allow intuitive filtering of data. To add them, we select the pivot table, go to *Insert > Slicer*, and choose the fields to be filtered. Value filters, on the other hand, allow us to show only those items that soddi- sfy a certain condition, for example, if we want to show only sales over €25,000.

We can also group data by time periods, such as days, months, or years, to perform a more effective chronological analysis. To enter temporal groupings, we select a field in the pivot table, then click *Pivot Table Tools > Analyze > Group Fields* and choose the grouping criteria, so by day, month, quarter, or year.

At this point we will be able to create any pivot table useful for our purpose. Let us try an exercise and a practical example at the same time to analyze monthly sales by product and region.

Let's start by organizing the data and make sure that columns A,B,C and D contain *Product, Region, Date of Sale* and *Sales Amount*, respectively. Now let's move on create the pivot table let's go to *Insert > Pivot Table* and select the data range. We· drag the *Product* field to the *Rows* area, the *Region field* to the *Columns* area, the *Sales Amount* field to the *Values* area (but make sure it is set to *Sum*) and finally drag the *Date of Sale* field to the *Filters* area (or use the *Group by Months* function).

The last step is to add a slicer by region: go to *Insert > Slicer* and select *Region* to quickly filter sales by geographic area.

The job is done: if we have followed the steps to the letter we may see a pivot table showing monthly sales broken down by product and region, with the possibility of filtering the data using Slicer or time filters.

7

COLLABORATION AND DATA SHARING IN EXCEL

In an increasingly connected work environment, the ability to collaborate and share data efficiently is fond- mental, which is why Excel offers several features to enable multiple users to work on the same file, protect sensitive data, share in the cloud, monitor changes, access permissions, integration with other applications, and automate information distribution processes.

Real-time file sharing

Real-time sharing allows multiple users to edit an Excel file simultaneously, reducing work time and improving productivity.With the integration of Excel with cloud platforms, such as OneDrive and SharePoint, this feature has become essential for teamwork both because it reduces the risk of file version conflicts and both because it gives us the ability to make instant changes visible to all participants.

To share a file in OneDrive, we start by saving the file, then go to *File > Save As* and choose a location on OneDrive. To share the file, we click *Share* in the upper right corner, enter the email addresses of collaborators, and set permissions (e.g., view-only or edit). Finally, we invite collaborators by simply pressing *Send*. If during collaboration we realize we need to change something, we can add comments directly to cells to discuss or provide instructions. To do this, we select a cell and click *Review > New Comment;* then, we write the comment and assign a mention using @name to notify a specific collaborator.

Monitoring changes

Excel offers tools to track changes made in a file, which is useful when multiple people are working on the same documents. To enable change tracking, we go to *Review > Share Workbook;* on the *Changes* tab, we check the *Keep track of changes* option and go to specify the details, i.e., the time interval for tracking and any changes on the screen or saving the log.

Of course, we can both view the changes, so we can see who edited a cell, when the change occurred, and what the previous value was, and restore old versions of the model. The latter function is very useful because, if an error is introduced, we can restore an earlier version of the file. To do this, go to *File > About > Version History*, select a version, and click *Restore*.

Data protection and security

When we share important files it is essential to protect sensitive data and ensure that only authorized people can access or make changes. If we want to **protect a worksheet**, we go to *Review > Protect Sheet*, set a password, and choose the actions allowed to other users who will be able to enter data, but not change the format.

To protect the entire workbook, go to *File > About > Protect Workbook* and choose one of the available options: *Mark as final,* to prevent further changes or *Encrypt with password* to require a password when opening.

If instead we want to restrict access to the data, we go to *File > Share > Grant Access* and set specific permissions e.g., view or edit only.

Integration with other tools

Excel can be integrated with other tools and applications to streamline workflow and improve data sharing. For example, Microsoft Teams enables collaboration on Excel files directly within the platform: simply upload an Excel file to a Teams channel and all team members can open and edit the file in real time.

Power BI, on the other hand, is an advanced tool for data visualization and analysis; it allows us to link our Excel files to Power BI to create dynamic dashboards. To do this, we simply save the Excel file to OneDrive or SharePoint, import the data into Power BI by going to *Power BI > Get Data > Excel File*, and finally create interactive visualizations based on the data in our file. A final integration is with Microsoft Flow, which allows us to automate processes such as notifications or sending reports-for example, it is useful if we want to automatically send an email with an Excel file that is updated every week.

Creating shareable reports

Excel offers several ways to share reports and analyses in formats suitable for distribution: to export to PDF we simply go to *File > Export > Create PDF/XPS*, choose a name and location for the file, and save it. We can also use advanced formatting and well-organized tables or add a header with a company logo. In addition, it will be possible to create dynamic links to Excel files saved in the cloud by simply sharing the file, in OneDrive or SharePoint, and then copying the link to allow others to access the updated document.

Automation and planning

To simplify data distribution, we can simply automate some processes. If we want to perform a scheduled update, we use Power Query to connect Excel to an external data source, such as a database, then configure an automatic update by going to *Data > Update All* and selecting a scheduled update option. If we want to automatically send a report instead, we save the file with a predefined format and then use a VBA script or a tool such as Power Automate to automatically send the file to a list of recipients.

8

MANAGEMENT OF LARGE DATASETS

Those who work systematically with Excel know how important it is to be able to work with a large amount of datasets; those who are still unfamiliar with the program, on the other hand, may need Excel for this very reason. Advanced features such as Power Pivot, Power Query, and optimization techniques make large datasets much easier to learn and use, especially since they allow you to work with large amounts of data in terms of volume and complexity.

Understanding the limitations of Excel

If we are faced with a large volume of data, we might immediately notice that Excel has inherent limitations on this type of work, an obstacle that can be easily overcome if we understand a few small tricks.

First of all, if the file is too large, Excel's performance may decrease: in fact, our pc's ability to handle large files depends on the available RAM and processor power. Excel supports up to
1,048,576 rows and 16,384 columns per worksheet (column inver- sion is 16384, so XFD). If we realize that Excel and its performance decreases, we can use some methods that can optimize efficiency while working with large datasets. Let's see which ones.

Optimization techniques in Excel - Using Power Pivot for data management.

One of the most effective tools for working with large volumes of data in Excel is Power Pivot, which is useful for working with complex data models and managing large datasets without compromising performance. The program allows us to analyze, process and load data from different sources more quickly and efficiently than the traditional spreadsheet. Power Pivot, in fact, allows us to work with millions of rows of data smoothly and without burdening Excel, and, thanks to the in-memory engine, it will be possible to perform complex calculations and analysis in less time.

First we need to load the data into Power Pivot, so we go to *Power Pivot> Manage* and load the data from external sources, but we can also use the program to pre-process the data before loading it into Power Pivot.

To create a relationship between tables instead, we use Power Pivot's *Diagram View* to define relationships between imported tables: thus we will have a centralized data model, which improves performance, avoiding duplications and optimizing calculations. Another possibility is given to us by DAX, a language that allows us to create advanced measures and calculations without loading the Excel worksheet: with the DAX language we can calculate aggregates such as sum, average, count, but also complex calculations such as profit margin calculation or forecasting future sales.

Using Power Query for data transformation

If we are looking for a tool for data preparation and cleaning, especially when working with large datasets, Power Query is the one for us because it allows us to import, transform and load data into Excel in an optimized way. The program allows us to automate the preparation of data, going to reduce the time needed for classic manual work, and allows us to manage complex datasets from different sources more easily.

To use Power Query we go to *Data > Get Data > From File* or *From Other Source* to load external data (CSV, Excel, database). In fact, the Power Query program gives us advanced options to filter, remove duplicate rows, merge tables, and change data types before loading data into Excel, but also to combine data from different sources without having to manage all directly into the Excel spreadsheet, thus greatly improving performance. We can also use the *Add Column* and *Remove Columns* function to reduce the volume of irrelevant data, thereby optimizing file management; and once the data have been transformed, load them into Power Pivot or directly into an Excel spreadsheet.

Avoid using too many volatile formulas

Volatile formulas, such as TODAY(), CASUAL(), and INDIRECT(), could significantly slow down Excel's performance, especially when used in a worksheet with large volumes of data, because these formulas are recalculated every time the worksheet is updated. It is preferable to use more stable formulas that do not continually update and to replace volatile formulas with static values, especially when the data do not need to be updated (so use the classic copy-and-paste as values); let's then preference matrix formulas, but beware: these formulas can only compromise performance if used excessively.

Data management techniques to improve performance
- Use Pivot Tables for efficient analysis

One of Excel's most powerful tools for data analysis is pivot tables, which are crucial when working with large volumes of data to synthesize and analyze information in more efficient way. Pivot tables reduce the workload in Excel by performing aggregate calculations without compro- puting performance and dynamically adapt to new data without requiring manual changes.

To create a pivot table, and analyze large datasets, we select our data and go to *Insert > Pivot Table.* Then we define the columns, rows, and values we want to analyze.At this point, we use the data filter to reduce the amount of information displayed and focus on the relevant data. Finally, we update the pivot table periodically, avoiding creating spreadsheets that rely on large, unnecessary cell ranges.

Using Excel files in .xlsb format.

When working with large datasets, the format of saving can affect the performance of the file: the .xlsb (Excel binary work- book) format is much more efficient than the .xlsx format, as it is compressed and significantly reduces the size of the file, in fact it has lower memory usage than the .xlsx format. and faster file opening and saving. To save a file in
.xlsb we go to *File > Save As,* select *Excel Binary Workbook (.xlsb)* in the file format drop-down menu, and finally save the file with the new format.

9

AUTOMATION AND PROJECTS IN EXCEL

One of the most powerful aspects of Excel is its ability to automate repetitive tasks, and creating customized solutions for business or analytical processes are some of the most important tasks Excel can support. With tools such as macros and the *Visual Basic for Applications* (VBA) language, we can develop projects that reduce manual workload and improve efficiency.

Introduction to macros

Macros are sequences of instructions recorded or written in VBA that automate repetitive operations in Excel: we can record a macro to automatically format a table, apply filters, perform calculations, or generate reports.

If, indeed, we want to record a macro, we go to the *Development* tab; if we have trouble finding it, let's enable it using this shortcut *File > Options > Customize Ribbon*. We then click on *Record Macro*, give the macro a name and choose a keyboard shortcut: now let's go and perform the operations we want to automate, for example, select cells, apply formulas or formatting; finally, click on *Stop Recording*.

If, on the other hand, we want to run a macro, we have two possibilities: the first is to go to *Development > Macros*, select the desired macro and click *Run*; the second is to use the key combination associated with the macro.

Despite their functionality, we may run into some limitations of recorded macros: they will not always be flexi- bile and may be complex to execute, especially at first. The advice, if we are faced with more complex automation, is to write VBA code.

Practical example:

We select a range of data, change the background color and apply bold; record and interrupt the macro, and then run the macro using the shortcut or via the Macro menu.

Introduction to VBA (Visual Basic for Applications)

If we need to create custom functions, intera- gire with Excel objects such as sheets and cells, or if we want to build custom user interfaces, we can use a programming language built into Excel that allows us to create all these advanced automations: the VBA.

To access the VBA editor, go to *Development > Visual Basic* or press Alt + F11. In the editor, we will see a tree structure representing the Excel project, such as the workbook, sheets or forms.

Forms contain VBA code: to add one, right-click on *VBA Project> Insert > Form*.

Excel objects, such as worksheets, cells, tables, and charts, are all objects that can be controlled with VBA.

Parameter configuration: Variable

declaration:

```
Dim nomeVariabile As Tipo
```

Example cycle:

```vba
For i = 1 To 10
    Cells(i, 1).Value = i
Next i
```

On-screen message:

```
MsgBox "Esempio di messaggio"
```

Writing a macro in VBA

Let's say we want to automatically format a table.

Next, we open the VBA editor (Alt+ F11), enter a form and write the following:

```vba
Sub FormatTable()
    Dim ws As Worksheet
    Set ws = ThisWorkbook.Sheets(1)
    With ws.Range("A1:D10")
        .Font.Bold = True
        .Interior.Color = RGB(200, 200, 255)
        .Borders.LineStyle = xlContinuous
    End With
End Sub
```

Finally, we return to Excel and run the macro.

Create a custom function with VBA

Custom Functions (or *UDFs*, User Defined Functions) expand Excel's calculation capabilities; among them, an estre- mely useful one is the calculation of VAT.

To do this, we always open the VBA editor, enter a form and write:

```vba
Function CalcolaIVA(importo As Double, aliquota As Double) As Double
    CalcolaIVA = importo * (1 + aliquota / 100)
End Function
```

So, let's go back to Excel and use the function in a cell:

```
=CalcolaIVA(100; 22).
```

Creation of forms and user interfaces

Excel allows us to create input forms through VBA to collect data or manage options.

If, for example, we want to create a user form to inse- re data, we go to *Insert > UserForm* in the VBA editor; add controls, such as text boxes and buttons, then associate the code with the button:

```vba
vba
Private Sub btnSubmit_Click()
    Dim nome As String
    nome = Me.txtNome.Value
    Sheets(1).Range("A1").Value = nome
    Unload Me
End Sub
```

Approach for automated projects

When we need to create a project with VBA, it is important to be able to follow all stages of development. Useful will be to follow this outline.

1. Project definition: we go on to identify the objectives, required inputs, and desired outputs. We can, for example, automate the weekly sales report by including calculation of key metrics, loading data from a CSV file, and generating graphs.

2. Planning: now we need to break down the project into smaller modules, such as calculations, report creation, and data import; then go on to define the logical flow of operations.

3. Development: at this point we can proceed with the creation of the macro and VBA: we write modular code, with subroutines for each part of the project, and use comments to document the code. An example of code for a report project is as follows:

```vba
Sub GeneraReport()
    Call ImportaDati
    Call CalcolaMetriche
    Call CreaGrafici
End Sub

Sub ImportaDati()
    ' Codice per importare dati
End Sub

Sub CalcolaMetriche()
    ' Codice per calcoli
End Sub

Sub CreaGrafici()
    ' Codice per grafici
End Sub
```

1. Testing: we go to verify, with some tests, each compo- nent separately: then, we run the complete design on a test dataset.

2. Deployment: we save the file as a *Workbook with macros enabled* (.xlsm). and protect the VBA code by going to *Tools > VBAProject Properties > Security*.

Best Practice in Automation

Some small tricks at this stage: we always try to document the code, using clear comments to explain what each part of the code does. We add checks to avoid irreversible changes, such as backing up data, so as to avoid operations that could compromise the work; we always evaluate and try to predict the adaptability of the project to new requirements. Finally, should we encounter one or more errors, we use code such as the following to handle them:

```vba
On Error GoTo GestioneErrore
' Codice
Exit Sub
GestioneErrore:
    MsgBox "Errore: " & Err.Description
End Sub
```

10

INTEGRATION OF EXCEL WITH OTHER TOOLS

Not just a spreadsheet but a powerful integration tool with other platforms, Excel can connect to databases, advanced analysis tools and reporting software, extending its capabilities for complex business scenarios.

Integration with Microsoft Access

Microsoft Access is a relational database that easily integrates with Excel, and with this connection, you will be able to import, export, and update data while maintaining a continuous flow between the two platforms.

To import data from Access to Excel, go to *Data > Retrieve and Transform > From Database > From Access Database* and select the .accdb or .mdb file then click *Import.*

Now we choose the tables or queries we want to upload and then just click *Upload* to transfer the data. If, on the other hand, we want to export data from Excel to Access, we first organize the data in Excel as a table, then open Access and choose *Import External Data > Excel Spreadsheet* then follow the wizard to map all the fields in the table.

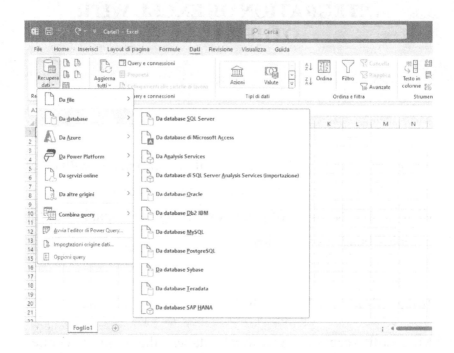

Practical example:

Suppose we have an Access database with monthly sales; we can create an Excel report that is automatically updated each month by linking directly to the "Sales" table.

Using Power Query

Power Query is an inte- grated data transformation tool in Excel that allows us to extract, transform, and load data (ETL); with Power Query, we will be able to merge two supplier databases with different formats and consolidate them into a single analyzable table.

In order to use it, we go to *Data > Retrieve and Transform* and choose a data source such as a CSV file or SQL database; then apply some transformations such as removing unnecessary columns, pivoting data or adding calculations, and finally load the processed data into Excel.

Integration with Power BI

Power BI is a business intelligence tool from Microsoft that integrates seamlessly with Excel.

The first step is to install the Power BI Publisher add-on: with the *Publish* button we can export tables or charts directly to Power BI. To do this we first save the Excel file to OneDrive or SharePoint; then move to Power BI, go to *Get Data > File > OneDrive*, and link the file. Finally, we create interat- tive dashboards based on the data.

Linking to external databases

Excel supports connections to databases such as SQL Server, MySQL, and Oracle via ODBC. To configure an ODBC connec- tion, we install the ODBC driver for the requested database; go to *Data> Retrieve and Transform> From Database*
> From SQL Server and enter the server address, creden- tial, and SQL query. An example of a SQL query embedded in Excel is as follows:

```
SELECT Nome, Cognome, Vendite
FROM Dipendenti
WHERE Vendite > 1000;
```

Thus, we can import the result directly into Excel and update the data with one click.

Practical example: using interactive Dashboards in Power BI for presentation, Power Pivot to create relational models, and Power Query to transform data let's try to create a monthly report, linking Excel to an Access database, and view it in Power BI; then use Power Query to clean and consolidate data from CSV files for later analysis with pivot tables.

11

INTEGRATION WITH PYTHON AND R

The integration of Excel with programming languages such as Python and R greatly expands our analytical and automation possibilities: these languages allow us to perform advanced analyses, create statistical models, and manage very large datasets, and understand how Excel can act as an interface to run Python and R scripts and configure these integrations.

How to use tools like the Python add-on for advanced data analysis

With Python, you can perform advanced analysis such as machine learning models, complex data processing, and creating custom visualizations.Excel allows you to integrate Python through tools such as xlwings, PyXLL, or the new native support introduced in Excel 365.

Configure Python in Excel

We start by installing Python from the python.org site, and then install useful libraries such as pandas, matplotlib, and openpyxl:

Bash

```
pip install pandas matplotlib openpyxl
```

To use Python natively in Excel, we open a spreadsheet and type in a Python formula using =PY(), with a function that will execute the Python code and return the result in the sheet, such as:

Excel

```
=PY("import    pandas    as    pd;    pd.DataFrame([[1,2],[3,4]],
columns=['A','B']).to_numpy()")
```

To use xlwings let's first install it:

Bash

```
pip install xlwings
```

Then we open Excel and activate the xlwings add-on, then create a Python script to interact with Excel:

```python
import xlwings as xw
wb = xw.Book()  # Connetti al file Excel aperto
sheet = wb.sheets[0]
sheet.range("A1").value = "Hello from Python"
```

Examples of advanced analysis with Python

To perform statistical analysis, we can use pandas and numpy to compute basic statistics on an Excel dataset.

```python
import pandas as pd
df = pd.read_excel("dati.xlsx")
print(df.describe())
```

To create of custom graphs, we will simply generate a graph in Python and enter it into Excel.

```python
import matplotlib.pyplot as plt
df['Vendite'].plot(kind='bar')
plt.savefig('grafico.png')
```

Using Excel as a frontend to run scripts in R or Python

To set integration with R, we start by downloading R from r-project.org and then installing libraries such as readxl and writexl:

```R
install.packages("readxl")
install.packages("writexl")
```

We can then read an Excel file:

```R
library(readxl)
dati <- read_excel("dati.xlsx")
summary(dati)
```

Or write an Excel file:

```R
library(writexl)
write_xlsx(dati, "output.xlsx")
```

If we want to use R-Excel integration with RExcel instead, we first install the RExcel extension to connect Excel and R in real time.

Practical examples of use

Automation, advanced analysis, and custom visualizations are just some of the benefits integration can bring us: automating complex workflows by combining the power of Python or R with the flexibility of Excel; performing calculations and analysis not available directly in Excel; and finally generating advanced charts not natively supported by Excel.

For example, we can use R to create a regression model and report the results in Excel.

```
R
model <- lm(Sales ~ MarketingSpend, data=dati)
summary(model)
```

Or, we can perform a cluster analysis using scikit- learn and write the results in Excel.

```
python
from sklearn.cluster import KMeans
import pandas as pd
df = pd.read_excel("dati.xlsx")
model = KMeans(n_clusters=3)
df['Cluster'] = model.fit_predict(df[['Vendite', 'Spese']])
df.to_excel("output_cluster.xlsx", index=False)
```

12

INTEGRATION WITH ERP SYSTEMS

An ERP (Enterprise Resource Planning) system is software used to manage business resources, such as sales, purchasing, accounting and production. Systems such as SAP, Oracle and Microsoft Dynamics allow large volumes of data to be collected. Excel still remains a fundamental tool for analyzing such information, but it can be integrated with ERP systems to effectively extract, analyze and present data.

Using Excel to extract and analyze data from SAP, Oracle, or other ERP systems

Integration between Excel and an ERP occurs through several methods. The first involves specific add-ins: some ERPs, such as SAP, offer add-ins for Excel. We have, for example, Oracle Smart View for Office, which allows you to connect to Oracle Hyperion data, or SAP Analysis for Microsoft Office, an add-in that allows queries on SAP data directly from Excel. The second method involves manually exporting data: many ERP systems allow reports to be exported in Excel or CSV format, allowing these files to be opened and analyzed in Excel. As a final method we find, once again, Power Query, which can be used to connect directly to the ERP system's database, or to set up an ODBC or OLE DB connection to extract data.

Steps to connect to an ERP database with Power Query

To connect to an ERP database with Power Query, we start by opening the program in Excel by going to *Data > Retrieve and Transform > From Database*. We then proceed by selecting the connection type, choosing *SQL Server database*; then, we enter the details of the ERP server and specify the server address, database name and, if neces- sary, the login credentials. As a final step, we import the data first by selecting the tables, or queries needed, and then wait for the data to be important in Excel for further analysis.

Practical example: we install the SAP Analysis for Office add-on; we open Excel and access the Analysis panel. Now, we run a query directly from SAP selectzioning the data view and defining parameters-the results will be displayed in Excel, ready to be analyzed with tools such as pivot tables and charts.

Automation of work flows

To automate workflows, we proceed by recording macros for repetitive processes: after configuring the data import, we record a macro to automate the process.

```vba
Sub CaricaDatiERP()
    ' Connessione a SAP tramite Analysis for Office
    Application.Run "SAPExecuteQuery", "NomeQuery"
End Sub
```

Finally, we configure a flow in Power Automate to download-care ERP reports and update them automatically in Excel.

Analysis of extracted data

Once the data have been obtained from the ERP system, Excel can be used to apply formulas for advanced calculations, thus to calculate profit margins, operating costs, or forecasts; to create pivot tables to summarize the data, such as analyzing sales by product, period, or region; and finally to visualize the data with advanced charts, using the combined charts or dashboards to present data clearly.

The integration of Excel with ERP allows us to enjoy many advantages, first of all automation, since with Power Query or VBA macros, it is possible to update ERP data in an automated way; users, then, can work on ERP data without having to access the system directly, and in addition Excel promises great flexibility, thanks to the possi- bility of customizing reports and analyses according to the needs of anyone who needs to use it.

13

INTEGRATION WITH MICROSOFT
TEAMS AND POWER AUTOMATE

In the corporate world, tools such as Microsoft Teams and Power Automate are becoming critical for collec- tion and workflow automation.

The integration of Excel with these tools allows everyday tasks, such as sharing reports or updating data, to be transformed into highly self-mated and efficient processes.

Integration with Microsoft Teams

Microsoft Teams is a collaborative tool for sharing files, initiating real-time conversations, and managing team projects. Excel can be easily inte- grated with Teams to simplify management access to shared data.

Sharing Excel files in Teams

To upload a file to a Teams channel, open Microsoft Teams and select a channel, then click *File > Upload* and choose the Excel file to share. Once uploaded, the file can be opened directly in Teams and initiate real-time collaboration so that multiple users can simultaneously edit the file, with the modi- fications synchronized.

Using Excel as a Tab in Teams

We start opening the desired channel in Teams, click + to add a new tab, select *Excel*, and choose a file from the shared repository-now the file will always be available as a tab for quick access.

Automated Notifications on Teams with Excel.

Using Power Automate, you can configure automatic notifications in Teams based on changes in Excel files. If we want to be notified of data updates, we open Power Automate and create a new flow. Now we set the trigger: *When a file is modified in OneDrive or SharePoint* and add an action: *Send a message in Teams*. We can also customize the message to include details of the changes, for example, "The file *Report2024.xlsx* has been updated."

Integration with Power Automate

Power Automate (formerly Microsoft Flow) allows you to create automated workflows between Excel and other strutures: this can include notifications, data transfers, and even automated analysis.

Automate notifications

Notifications can be set up to alert users whenever a specific condition is met in an Excel file. For example, we can decide to have an e-mail sent when a value exceeds a threshold. To do this, we open Power Automate and create a new flow by selecting the *Edit File* trigger *in OneDrive*. Now, we add an action to check the values in the Excel file: we use the *Get rows from a worksheet* action to read the data and configure a condition: for example, "If *Total Sales* column > 20,000." Finally, we go on to add the *Send an e-mail* action to notify the user.

Automated data update

Power Automate can be used to synchronize data between Excel and other applications, such as an SQL database or a sales management app. If we want to transfer data from Excel to a database, we first configure the *When an Excel file is updated* trigger and use the action

Insert rows in SQL to transfer the new data to the database. Finally, we schedule the flow to perform the operation every day or every week.

Creation of complex flowsof work

With Power Automate it is possible to create multi-step processes that combine notifications, data transfers, and automations. For example, if we need to handle approval requests, the trigger will be *New Request Added in Excel* which will be followed by several possible actions, such as: *Send an approval request* in Teams; if approved, *Add the request to an SQL table*; if rejected, send an email to the requester with the reasons for rejection.

14

EXCEL NEW FEATURES GUIDE FOR OFFICE 2025

With the latest version of Office 2025, Excel has enhanced its functionality by introducing new dynamic functions and linked data types, making data management more flexible and interactive. These innovations make it possible to transform simple spreadsheets into advanced tools for analysis, report creation, and automation of daily tasks. We will now understand how to make the most of these new features to optimize work with data, from managing dynamic arrays to creating interactive reports and inte- grating with external data sources.

Dynamic functions and dynamic arrays

Dynamic Functions allow multiple cells to be automatically filled with a single result, without the need to

Copying the formula manually. These functions automatically adapt to changing data, creating dynamic and interactive reports.

Main dynamic functions

1. SEQUENCE

Generates a series of numbers ordered in a specified range.

Parameter configuration:

```
SEQUENZA(righe; colonne; inizio; passo)
```

Example:

```
Excel
=SEQUENZA(5; 1; 1; 1)
```

This will create a column with the numbers 1 to 5.

2. UNIQUE

Returns a list of unique values from a range, eliminating duplicates.

Parameter configuration:

```
UNICO(array)
```

Example:

```
Excel
=UNICO(A1:A10)
```

This will list all unique names in the range A1:A10.

3. FILTER

Filters data according to a specific criterion.

Parameter configuration:

```
FILTRA(array; includi; [se_vuoto])
```

Example:

```
Excel
=FILTRA(B1:B10; A1:A10="Italia"; "Nessun risultato")
```

It will return the sales in B1:B10 associated with the value "Italy" in A1:A10.

4. ORDER

Sorts a range of data according to a defined criterion.

Parameter configuration:

```
ORDINA(array; [indice_ordinamento]; [ordine])
```

Example:

```
Excel
=ORDINA(A1:A10; 1; 1)
```

It will sort the range in ascending order.

Creation of dynamic and customized reports

With Dynamic Functions it is possible to create interactive and automated reports. Let's look at an example of a report with the UNIQUE and SUM.SE functions. In the range A1:A10 are the names of the salespeople and in B1:B10 are the sales. To create the report we use =UNICO(A1:A10) to list the unique sellers and
=SUM.IF(A1:A10; D1; B1:B10) to calculate the total sales for each seller, where **D1** is the unique seller. As a result we will get an automatic summary of sales for each seller without having to manually update the list.

- - -

Geographic and data functions

Excel 2025 also introduces the ability to use Linked Data Types, which provide access to external information in real time; a particularly useful feature for geographic and economic data.

Geographic data allow us to integrate information such as population, area, or GDP of a given location. To do this, we enter a location, such as "Italy," into a cell, then go to *Data > Geography* to convert it to a geogra- phic data type; then, we use the formula =B1.Population to get the population of that location.

Instead, it is possible to link financial data in Excel to acce- date up-to-date information on stocks, exchange rates, and economic indicators. Let's try entering a stock symbol, such as "MSFT" for Microsoft; then select *Data > Stocks* to transform the text into a financial data type. Finally, we use =B1.Price to display the current stock price.

Automation with Linked Data

With **Linked Data Types**, complex processes can be automated by combining real-time updated data and dynamic formulas. Suppose we want to monitor the economic performance of several nations: we enter the names of the nations in A1:A10, we transform the cells into geographic data types, then create a table with Population, GDP and Area using dynamic formulas, e.g. =A1.GDP to obtain GDP. This combination makes Excel a powerful tool for business intelligence and data analysis.

15

CUSTOMIZATION OF EXCEL

Customizing Excel is key to optimizing workflow and tailoring the work environment to your specific needs. Through tools such as the custom multi-function bar, add-ons, and scripts, you can transform Excel into a system tailored for complex analysis and operations.

Custom multifunction bar

The Excel ribbon, located at the top of the interface, can be customized to include the most frequently used functions and commands, improving efficiency.

To customize the ribbon, let's start by adding custom commands: go to *File> Options*
> Multifunction bar *customization*. In the window that comes up

opens, select a command from the left-hand list, choose an existing tab, or create a new one, and click *Add*.

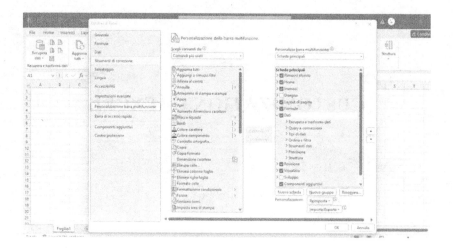

To create a custom tab, we click *New Tab* in the same window: now: rename the tab with a meaningful name, such as "Data Analysis," and then add the desired commands. Once the customization is complete, we can save and export the configuration file to share with other users.

Practical example:

Let's try to create a data analysis tab. We add commands such as Pivot Tables, Advanced Charts and Filters to the custom tab; then, rename the tab to "Data Analysis," then save the changes and verify the custom tab in the ribbon.

Custom add-ons

Add-ons, or add-ins, extend the functionality of Excel by adding advanced tools developed by Microsoft or third parties.

To install an add-on, we go to *Insert > Add-ons*: we can now access the store and search for the desired component. Eventually, we will just click *Add* to install it.

With a few programming basics, we can also create an add-on with VBA or use the more advanced tools such as JavaScript API for Office.

To create a component with VBA, we start by developing a VBA form that performs a series of auto- matized operations: then we save the file as an Excel add-on (.xlam) and activate the component in *File > Options > Add-ons > Go.*

To create a custom function with VBA add-in, we use the following code:

```vba
Function ConvertiEuro(Dollari As Double) As Double
    ConvertiEuro = Dollari * 0.85
End Function
```

Eventually, we will just save the file as .xlam and enable the component.

Links to Office scripts

Office Scripts are scripts executed in the cloud via Excel Online, ideal for automating repetitive tasks. To create one, we access from *Automation > Record Action* in Excel Online; complete the task, such as formatting data or creating a chart, then save the script and assign it a name. Scripts can be run directly in Excel Online or through integrations with Power Automate to automate workflows.

Practical example:

Let us now try to create a script for formatting data. The first step is to record a script that: adds an automatic filter, applies a table format to a range, and changes the color of cells with values above a certain threshold. Eventually, by saving the script, we could reuse it whenever we need to work with similar data.

16

TOOLS FOR DATA VALIDATION

Data validation in Excel is essential to ensure the accuracy and integrity of information in worksheets. Through advanced controls and specific techniques, errors can be prevented, structured inputs can be created, and large datasets can be compared efficiently.

Advanced controls - Create dynamic and interactive drop-down menus

A drop-down menu allows users to select a value from a predefined list, reducing input errors. To create a static drop-down menu, we select the cells in which we want to insert the menu, then go to *Data*
> *Validate Data*. In the window, we choose *List* as the validation criteria and enter the values separated by a

comma, such as "Yes, No, Maybe," or we connect an inter- vall of cells containing the values.

Instead, to create a dynamic drop-down menu we have two options: either create a dynamic table or define a name for the dynamic range. In the first case, we enter the values in a range and turn them into a table with *Ctrl*
+ *T*. In the second, we define a name for the dyna- mic interval by going to *Formulas > Name Management > New Name*. Then we use a formula like the following:

```Excel
=SCARTO(Tabella1[Colonna], 0, 0,CONTA.VALORI(Tabella1[Colonna]))
```

Finally, we apply data validation using the name defined as a reference for the list.

Practical example:

Suppose a company wants to create a drop-down menu to select available regions, such as North, Central, and South, based on automatically updated values. Let's enter the regions in a table called "Regions"; create a dynamic range and apply the drop-down menu with data validation.

Data validation with custom formulas

Custom formulas allow advanced rules to be applied during data entry.

We can, for example, **limit entry to speci- fic values** by instructing the user to enter only integers greater than 10. To do this, we start by selecting cells, go to *Data > Data Validation*, choose *Custom* as the criterion, and use the formula:

```
Excel
```
```
=E(A1>10, INT(A1)=A1)
```

If instead we want to avoid duplicates by ordering that the values in the column must be unique, we select the range and use the following formula:

```
Excel
```
```
=CONTA.SE($A$1:$A$100, A1)=1
```

Data Reconciliation

Data reconciliation allows you to compare two datasets to identify discrepancies or duplicates. Techniques for comparing large datasets are based on the use of formulas, pivot tables, or Power Query.

With Pivot Tables, the converse is very simple: just create two pivot tables based on the datasets and compare the totals or use calculated fields to analyze the differences. Same simplicity with Power Query: load the datasets, use the *Merge Query* option to merge the tables, and finally

We filter out missing rows or duplicates. For example, if a finance department needs to check whether the transactions in an Excel file match the data in the management system, we simply import the two datasets into Power Query, merge the data based on a key field, such as Transaction ID, and finally identify the rows that do not match.

The use of formulas, on the other hand, is, yes, simple, but it requires some precautions.

The formula **COMPARE**, is used to check whether a value in one dataset exists in another:

Excel

```
=SE(È.NUMERO(CONFRONTA(A2,Foglio2!$A$1:$A$100,0)),"Presente","Assente")
```

The formula COUNT.**IF**, is used to count the occurrences of a value:

Excel

```
=CONTA.SE(Foglio2!$A$1:$A$100, A2)
```

The formula **DIFFERENCE BETWEEN TWO TABLES**, on the other hand, is used to compare two tables to find unique values:

Excel

```
=SE(VAL.NON.DISP(CONFRONTA(A2,  Foglio2!$A$1:$A$100,  0)),  "Unico",
"Duplicato")
```

17

VBA DEBUGGING AND OPTIMIZATION

Visual Basic for Applications (VBA) is a powerful tool for automating processes and creating custom solutions in Excel. However, as in any programming language, VBA code may contain errors or inefficiencies.

Debugging tools in VBA

Debugging means identifying and correcting errors in code, and Excel VBA provides built-in tools to simplify this process.

Use of Breakpoints

A breakpoint stops code execution at a specific point, allowing you to examine it in detail. To impo-

stand a breakpoint, we open the VBA Editor with the shortcut *Alt + F11*. We place the cursor on the line of code where we want the breakpoint, press *F9* or click in the gray bar to the left of the line.

An example code is as follows:

```vba
Sub SommaValori()
    Dim somma As Double
    Dim i As Integer
    For i = 1 To 10
        somma = somma + Cells(i, 1).Value
    Next i
    MsgBox somma
End Sub
```

If we want to check the sum value during each itera- tion, we only need to import a breakpoint on:

```
somma = somma + Cells(i, 1).Value.
```

Immediate Window

The Immediate Window allows you to execute commands and visua- lize values while debugging. To use it we press *Ctrl + G* to open it and type a command, such as:

```vba
? Cells(1, 1).Value
```

This returns the value of cell A1. If during debugging we want to check the state of a variable, and find the value that will appear in the Immediate Window, we use:

```vba
Debug.Print somma
```

Watch Window

The Watch Window allows you to monitor variables and properties during execution; to set it up, we select a varia- bile in the code; right-click and choose *Add Watch*, then specify a condition, such as when a variable changes. This way we will be able to quickly identify unexpected conditions and can observe values in real time.

Step Through (F8)

With the *F8* key, we can run the code line by line and analyze the flow.

VBA code optimization

VBA code performance is critical for handling complex worksheets and large datasets-let's look at some techniques that will help us reduce execution time.

Avoiding inefficient loops

If not optimized, loops can significantly slow down execution; the following is an example of an inef- ficient loop:

```vba
For i = 1 To 1000
    For j = 1 To 1000
        Cells(i, j).Value = i * j
    Next j
Next i
```

To get around this problem we will use arrays, which allow us to process data in memory before writing them to the sheet.

```vba
Dim dati() As Double
ReDim dati(1 To 1000, 1 To 1000)

For i = 1 To 1000
    For j = 1 To 1000
        dati(i, j) = i * j
    Next j
Next i
Range("A1:J1000").Value = dati
```

Reduce the use of Select and Activate

To avoid incurring a slowdown during execution, we must avoid selecting or activating cells unnecessarily. The following is an inefficient example:

```vba
Range("A1").Select
ActiveCell.Value = "Testo"
```

The solution will be as follows:

```vba
Range("A1").Value = "Testo"
```

Disable screen updates

When running macros, Excel updates the screen for each change, slowing down the process. To solve this problem, we use *Application.ScreenUpdating:*

```vba
Application.ScreenUpdating = False
' Codice della macro
Application.ScreenUpdating = True
```

Manual calculation

If we do not want Excel to update the formulas at each , we can import the manual calculation:

```vba
Application.Calculation = xlCalculationManual
' Codice della macro
Application.Calculation = xlCalculationAutomatic
```

Avoid Variant Variables

Variables of type Variant take up more memory and slow down execution; better to always declare the type of the variable:

```vba
Dim somma As Double
```

Reduce the use of volatile functions

Volatile functions in Excel are functions that automatically recalculate every time a change is made to the worksheet, whether or not their argo- ments have changed. This can negatively affect file performance, especially when working with large or complex sheets. Some of the most common volatile functions include:

- *NOW()*, which returns the current date and time;

- *CASUAL()*, which generates a random number between 0 and 1;

- *CASUAL.TRA()*, which generates a random number within a specified range;

- *INDIRECT()*, which returns a reference specified as text;

- *TODAY()*, which returns the current date without the time;

- *MOVE()*, which returns a reference to a range shifted relative to a specific cell.

Whenever Excel recalculates a worksheet, all volatile functions are recalculated, even if they have not been changed, and this can significantly slow down operations. With complex or very large sheets, intensive use of volatile functions can cause high CPU usage and memory, reducing overall performance. In addition, because these functions are constantly recalculating, the derived data can change continuously, making it difficult to track or stabilize the results.

Volatile functions can be powerful tools in Excel, but their use must be balanced with the need to maintain worksheet performance. To reduce the use of volatile functions, we can proceed in four different ways.

1. Replace with Nonvolatile Functions

We use alternative formulas that do not automatically recalculate. Thus, to replace *TODAY()* or *NOW()*, we manually enter the date/time or use *CTRL* +; for the date or *CTRL* + *SHIFT* +; for the time.

2. Blocking Manual Recalculation

To avoid constant recalculations, you can copy the result of the volatile function and paste it as a value:

```
Excel
=OGGI() → Copia → Incolla Speciale → Valori
```

3. Using Custom Functions with VBA

We can create macros that calculate only when needed:

```vba
Function DataFissa() As Date
    DataFissa = Date
End Function
```

4. Using Manual Calculation

Let's go to *File > Options > Formulas* and select *Manual Calculation* to avoid continuous recalculation; next- mind we can update manually by pressing *F9*.

Volatile functions are useful with Interactive Dashboards, when a real-time update is needed, or with simulation models, when random values need to be generated for scenario analysis.

18

PRACTICAL APPLICATIONS OF EXCEL IN SPECIFIC AREAS

Excel is not just a calculation software: it is a versatile platform used in almost every sector data management and ana- lysis. That is why today you cannot avoid knowing how to use Excel in finance, production, marketing and even human resources, the software being a concrete and practical help in solving complex problems and optimizing processes.

Finance: budget creation, budget analysis, investment management

In the financial arena, Excel allows us to create budgets, analyze budgets, and even intelligently manage our investments. First, it allows us to create comprehensive budget models, integrating forecasts of income and expenses. Key features include in this area are: the logical functions, such as SE and SOMMA.SE, to calculate variances and variances; dynamic graphs, which visi- vely represent budget distribution; and also our cherished pivot tables, which analyze expenses and revenues divided by categories for us.

Practical example:

A business can construct a spreadsheet with estimated month-to-month income in A1:A12 and expenses in B1:B12. To calculate the monthly balance, simply use this code and then create a bar graph to display a comparison of income and expenses in a calendar month:

```
Excel
=A1-B1
```

With budget analysis, Excel allows us to monitor financial performance in real time; this is thanks to conditional formatting, which highlights critical values such as might be results that go below a certain threshold, and also statistical functions, such as AVERAGE, VAR.P, and DEV.ST, used to assess data dispersion. For example, we could analyze a quarterly budget with a pivot table to filter cost categories more quickly and determine areas of overspending.

Finally, Excel allows us to better manage our investment portfolio through financial functions, such as TIR, the

Internal Rate of Return, and CURRENT.VAL, which calcolate for us the net present value of investments, and thanks to the famous function SEARCH.VERT that extracts updated financial data from a sheet or external source.

Production: inventory management, resource planning

In the production sphere, Excel allows us to monitor the inventory accurately thanks to the CONTA.SE function, which determines the quantity of products available, and thanks to the dynamic tables, used to automatically update stock levels. If, on the other hand, we simply want to plan our company's resources, we will use the DATE and TIME time functions to track deadlines or Gantt Charts, to manage projects.

Practical example:

Suppose we want to create a dashboard to monitor business expenses using dynamic graphs, to visualize the an- dament of expenses over time, Slicer, to quickly filter data by department or month, and pivot tables to summarize expenses by category. We begin by collecting the expenditure data in a table, e.g., A1:D100; prose- guise by creating a pivot table and adding filters by department; finally, we will go on to insert a pie chart showing the percentage of expenditure for each department.

Marketing: sales analysis, campaign management, KPI reporting

In the broad world of marketing, Excel can be useful when we find ourselves needing to analyze sales, manage promotional or adv campaigns, or even to analyze KPI reports.

Sales can be tracked by combined graphs, comparing sales with targets, or by segmentations based on a particular geographic area, product, or time period (days, months, years). For example, we will be able to create a table with monthly sales by region and use the SUMMA.SE function to calculate total sales for each region, simply using this code:

```
Excel
=SOMMA.SE(A1:A100; "Nord"; B1:B100)
```

Campaign management and analysis of KPI reports are greatly simplified. The former, can be enjoyed mediate simple tables, which list planned activities, channels used and budget, or through Power Query, which imports data from marketing platforms, such as Google Analytics, and transforms it into useful insights. The second ones, on the other hand, are concerned with measuring performance with line graphs, which display trends in key KPIs, or through Slicer and Timeline, embedded in pivot tables, which create interattive filters and monitor results over the long term.

Human resources: payroll management, attendance analysis

How many times have we found ourselves having to process an employee's reimbursement plans, manage the timesheet or simple absences? In HR Excel has meant a surge into the future, making managers more active, fast and functional.

Excel allows us to calculate paychecks using logical functions, which calculate taxes and contributions, and sheet protection, which provides security for all sensitive data that will be entered. If, in fact, we wanted to calculate the net amount of a paycheck, we would simply use the following code:

```
Excel
=SALARIO_BRUTTO - (SALARIO_BRUTTO * ALIQUOTA_FISCALE)
```

If, on the other hand, we were to monitor absenteeism and hours worked, we would use conditional formatting in Excel, which highlights days of absence, and scatter plots, which would represent weekly employee attendance data.

19

LITTLE-KNOWN BUT POWERFUL EXCEL FUNCTIONS

Excel continues to evolve with introducing advanced functions that improve the efficiency and flexibility of working with data: in particular three advanced functions that are XLOOKUP, LET and LAMBDA, represent powerful tools to simplify data management and create custom formulas without the use of VBA. These functions represent a step forward for Excel users, offering greater efficiency and customization: the first, simplifies and enhances searches, the second reduces the complexity of formulas, and the last allows custom functions to be created directly in the sheet.

XLOOKUP: the evolution of CERCA.VERT.

XLOOKUP is an advanced search function introduced to replace SEARCH.**VERT** and **SEARCH.ORIZZ**. It is more flexible and solves many limitations of the previous functions, such as the

difficulty of searching to the left and the requirement of an ordinal interval. Compared with SEARCH.VERT, this function can search left, does not require an ordered range, and supports exact and approximate corri- spondences.

Parameter configuration:

```
Excel

=XLOOKUP(valore;intervallo_cerca;intervallo_ritorno;[valore_no
n_trovato]; [modalità_corrispondenza]; [modalità_ricerca])
```

Let's try to analyze its structure: value is the item to be searched, range_search that range in which to search for the value, range_return: that from which to return results, value_not_found *(optional)* is the value to be returned if the search is unsuccessful, match_mode *(optional)* is type of exact or approximate match, and finally search_mode, also optional, is the direction of the search which can go from the top or the bottom.

Practical example:

Suppose we have a table with the names of employees in A2:A10 and their salaries in B2:B10. To search for the salary of a specific employee, we can use a function that will return the salary associated with "Luigi Bianchi" or "Not found" if the name does not exist:

```
Excel

=XLOOKUP("Luigi Bianchi"; A2:A10; B2:B10; "Non trovato")
```

LET: simplification of complex formulas

The LET function allows names to be assigned to inter- average results in formulas, making the calculation clearer and optimizing performance because Excel calculates values only once. This feature improves the readability of more complex formulas and reduces the number of repeated calculations, so performance is improved.

Parameter configuration:

Excel
```
=LET(nome1; valore1; [nome2; valore2]; ...; calcolo_finale)
```

The name of the first assigned value is name1:, value1 is the value or calculation associated with name1, finally the formula that uses the assigned values is final_calculation.

Practical example:

We calculate profit margin with less repetition of calculations, assigning names to sales and costs so as to reduce repetition and improve readability.

Excel
```
=LET(vendite; A1; costi; B1; margine; vendite - costi; margine
/ vendite)
```

LAMBDA: create custom functions without VBA

LAMBDA allows you to create custom functions in Excel without having to use VBA or scripts.

It is particularly useful for defining recurring formulas, which can be used multiple times in the worksheet; it also allows for complete customization without the use of VBA, for reuse because, once defined, the function can be used anywhere in the file, and finally, because it does not require the use of macros, it reduces security risks.

Parameter configuration:

Excel

```
Excel
=LAMBDA(parametro1; parametro2; ...; calcolo)
```

The input values of the function are parameter1, parameter2 while the calculation is the formula that defines the function.

Practical example:

Suppose we want to create a function that calculates the square of a number.

```
Excel
=LAMBDA(x; x^2)
```

After defining this function, we can use it for any value:

```
Excel
=Quadrato(5)  → Risultato: 25
```

To save and reuse LAMBDA: we go to *Formulas > Name Management*, create a new name and assign the LAMBDA function, and finally use the name defined anywhere on the sheet.

20

TIPS FOR COLLABORATION AND SHARING IN EXCEL

Excel is a powerful software not only for data analysis and management, but also for collaboration and sharing. Whether we work in a team or simply want to share a file with others, it is essential to know the options for facilitating real-time collaboration and ensuring data security. To collaborate and to manage sheet protection and data security permissions, Excel gifts us with two powerful tools: SharePoint and OneDrive. By combining these two tools, Excel gives us powerful functionality to collaborate in real time and to share files a totally secure way. Careful management of permissions, and protection of spreadsheets, will enable us to work safely at all times, reducing any risk of leakage of sensitive data, changes to files, or any other problems that might arise in the workplace, so that work between teams and companies is always functional and secure.

Collaborate in real time with SharePoint

SharePoint is a collaboration platform for securely storing, organizing and sharing files, particularly useful for teams working on joint projects. Using the pairing of Excel and SharePoint we will be able to create and store Excel files in a SharePoint docu- ments library, allowing team members to access, edit, and comment on them simultaneously; control all versions, because SharePoint keeps track of the modi- fications made to the file, allowing us to see who has modified what and restore previous versions if necessary; and finally also easily share the Excel file with team members, and manage permissions for who can view, edit, or comment on the document.

Practical example:

If we are working on a corporate budget plan with our team, we can upload the Excel file to SharePoint. Each team member will be able to edit items related to their responsibilities, such as income and expenses, in real time. The changes will be visible to everyone immediately, improving collaboration and efficiency.

Collaboration with OneDrive

OneDrive is another cloud storage tool from Microsoft, which seamlessly integrates Excel for sharing and collaboration. We can upload our Excel file to OneDrive and share it with other people, allowing real-time modifications. OneDrive allows us to access files anywhere, whether on desktops, tablets, or smartphones, and at any time: thanks to direct sharing, we can send a link to the Excel file, or invite specific users to edit it, and simultaneously operate on the same file without editing conflicts, thanks to real-time synchronization.

Practical example:

Imagine we are a sales manager and we want to update a monthly report in Excel together with our marketing team. We upload the file to OneDrive, conce- access to team members, and everyone can make changes, such as entering new sales or updating performance metrics.

Management of sheet protection and data security permissions

One of the darkest spots when working online or on the web concerns data protection-how do we make it 100 percent secure when working on an Excel file? Today's program offers several options to protect , manage auto-releases, and ensure that only authorized people can make changes.

To protect worksheets, we can use func- tions that allow us to prevent accidental or unauthorized changes to the contents of the sheet. The level of protection can be applied to cells, rows, columns, and even the entire file.

To protect the sheet we go to *Review > Protect Sheet* and add a password to prevent modification of the sheet: we can choose to allow only certain actions e.g., allow cell selection, but prevent data modification.

Practical example:

We are creating a budget model and do not want users to modify certain cells, such as those containing formulas; we can then protect the sheet so that only selected cells can be modified. This will prevent other people from accidentally editing critical data.

Permissions management and file sharing

When we need to share an Excel file, it is important to manage permissions so that only the right people can access, view or edit the document. The options for managing permissions depend on where we store the file. When we authorize with SharePoint or OneDrive, we can decide whether to allow users to view or edit the file: to avoid acci- dent changes, it is best to allow only viewing and limit editing permissions. We can also invite selected members of our team and assign different permissions: some might only have permission to edit, while others have permission to comment; finally, it is always best to set a password to protect against unauthorized access to the file.

Practical example:

Suppose we want to share a monthly report with our team, but we want to prevent accidental changes from being made to the formula columns. We upload the file to OneDrive, grant read access to the team, and authorize only senior members to make changes.

Monitoring changes and comments

Excel allows us to track changes and add comments to cells, which is especially useful when multiple people are working on the same document. The program keeps track of changes when the file is saved to SharePoint or OneDrive-so it will always be possible to see who made what changes and perhaps restore an earlier version of the file. In addition, it will always be possible to add comments and notes to cells so that instructions and explanations can be provided to those who are working on the file: comments will be visible to those who have access to the file and can be useful for explaining context or discussing specific points.

Practical example:

Suppose we are collaborating with a colleague on a sales forecast; we can add a comment to a cell containing an important piece of data, indicating the reason for a particular projection or suggesting a change.

21

CONCLUSION

The power of Excel in daily and professional life

Excel is not just a tool: it is a gateway to a world of possibilities. Throughout this book, we have expllo- rated every aspect of this remarkable software, starting with its basics and ending with more advanced techniques for automating processes and integrating Excel with external tools. Now that we have reached the conclusion, it is important to reflect on why Excel represents a key compe- tence in the modern landscape and the value it can add not only to work, but also to personal life.

Today, the ability to analyze data, automate processes and present information effectively is one of the most in-demand skills in almost every industry. From finance to marketing, from engineering to healthcare, Excel is a universal platform that brings together very professional figures. Excel is not limited to being a simple spreadsheet. With its advanced functions, macros, and integration with tools such as Power Query, Power BI, and programming languages such as Python, it becomes a hub for data management, processing, and visualization. This versatility makes it an irreplaceable tool for analysts, managers and developers. Knowing Excel means knowing how to work smarter, not harder. Automating repetitive tasks, creating forecasting models or generating interactive reports saves valuable time that can be reinvested in strategic activities. Despite technological evolution and the advent of more complex tools, Excel remains the software of choice because of its widespread use and user-friendly interface. Most companies use it as standard, making this skill a fundamental prerequisite for anyone who wants to be competitive in the business world.

Although often associated with work, Excel can significantly improve your personal life: you can create monthly budgets, track expenses, and plan your savings. With tools such as pivot tables and dina- mic charts, you can quickly visualize areas where you can save or optimize your finances. Excel is perfect for planning events, creating customized calendars or orga- nizing trips: we can develop comparison tables between costs and routes, keeping everything under control in one file. Whether it's fitness, reading or study goals, Excel allows us to track our progress by using charts to visualize our achievements and create a feed-back system that motivates us to reach our goals. But Excel can be used to plan renovations, manage household inventories or even organize personal collections such as books, movies or video games.

Knowing how to use Excel gives us a unique advantage: the ability to transform data into meaningful information. We live in an age when data is everywhere, and the ability to interpret it is an incredible power. From a simple list of contacts to a complex database, Excel allows us to bring order to chaos, analyze trends, and make infor- mated decisions. Learning Excel is not just about learning a stru- ment: it means adopting a new way of thinking because it teaches us to break down problems, find creative solutions and optimize processes. This mindset is applicable to every area of life, making us more organized, efficient and proactive people. As we have seen, Excel is constantly evolving. Functions such as UNIQUE, SEQUENCE and FILTER did not exist a few years ago, and the software will conti- nuously improve with time. Keeping curiosity alive and updating regularly is critical to taking full advantage of Excel's potential.

Challenger: learn Excel in 30 days

And now, to conclude our study let's try a challenge: to become an Excel expert in 30 days. With the knowledge in this guide and training, it will be possi- ble to acquire solid skills that will change the way we work with Excel and all its many useful features.

• Week 1: Basics

The goal is to be able to create a neat spreadsheet with basic formulas. Skill to be achieved will be familiarizing with the Excel interface, learning how to enter and format data, and finally practicing simple formulas such as SUM, AVERAGE, and IF.

• Week 2: Intermediate functions and data analysis

The goal is to create an analytical report with pivot tables and graphs. The skills to be achieved will be delving into logical functions (IF, AND, OR), learning to use text and search functions (SEARCH.VERT, INDEX, COMPARE), and finally practicing with pivot tables and dynamic graphs.

• Week 3: Advanced functions and automation

The goal is to automate a repetitive process using VBA or to create an advanced analysis model. The skills to be conquered will be the study of Power Query and Power Pivot, introduction to automation with macros and VBA, and finally knowing how to experiment with integrating Excel with other tools such as Power BI or Access.

- Week 4: Custom projects

The goal is to complete a complex project that demonstrates mastery of Excel. The skills to be achieved will be the application of what has been learned by transferring it to a real-world project, such as conducting a business data analysis or a simple personal budget report; exploring advanced features such as SEQUENCE, UNIQUE and FILTER; and finally designing an interactive dashboard.

A multifunctional tool always at hand: here is Excel, more than a software and more than a workout, it will really be our trusted companion for any need in our lives, from the most complex problems to the organization of the private and work sphere. Because those who said Excel is too complex are wrong: no matter where you start, the path to becoming an Excel expert is accessible to anyone willing to invest time and effort.

Now is the time to take up the challenge and find out all we can do with Excel.

CONGRATULATIONS! THANK YOU FOR READING MY MANUAL. AS PROMISED, HERE ARE THE ADDITIONAL **BONUS** TO REDEEM:

EXCEL VIDEO COURSE FOR BEGINNERS WITH OVER 12+HOURS:

22

FULL GLOSSARY OF EXCEL

This glossary is designed so that it will be a practical and immediate reference point for mastering Excel concepts, features, and commands. You can use it while studying this guide and return to it whenever you encounter a term or concept that is still unclear to you.

A

Absolute Reference_Reference: a reference to a cell that remains constant when copied or moved; it is denoted by the symbol $, e.g., $B$2.

Active Cell_Cell: the selected cell you are working on, and is highlighted by a thick border.

Algorithm_Algorithm: a sequence of steps used to solve problems or perform calculations.

Array_Matrix: array, static or dynamic, is a group of values that can be treated as a single unit in formulas or functions.

AutoCorrect_Correction: a function that automatically corrects typos or replaces abbreviations with full words.

AutoFilter_Filter: a feature that allows you to filter the data in a table according to specific criteria.

AutoRecover_AutoRecover: a function that automatically saves the document to prevent data loss in case of sudden closure.

AutoSum_SUM: The command that auto-inserts the SUM function to calculate the total of a range of cells.

B

Bar Chart_Bar Chart: a type of chart that uses horizontal bars to represent data.

Binary Workbook_File Excel (.xlsb): a file format that allows workbooks to be saved with reduced size and faster loading times than the standard .xlsx format.

Breakpoints_Points: the debugging tool in VBA that interrupts code execution at a specific point to analyze behavior.

C

Cell Address_Cell Address: the unique location of a cell in a sheet, defined by the combination of column letter and row number (e.g., A1).

Cell_Cell: the basic unit of a worksheet, defined by the intersection of a row and a column.

Chart_Graph: the visual representation of data, such as pie, bar, or line graphs.

Circular Reference_Reference: an error that occurs when a formula refers to itself directly or indirectly.

Clustered Column Chart_Clustered Column Chart: data visualization in which columns represent values grouped by category.

Column_Column: a vertical series of cells identified by letters, e.g., A, B, C.

Conditional Formatting_Formatting: the instrument that changes the appearance of cells based on specific criteria.

CSV_File CSV: Comma Separated Values file format, used to save tabular data as plain text sepa- rted by commas or other delimiters.

D

Dashboard: a set of graphs, tables, and interactive visualizations used to succinctly represent data.

Data Model_Model: structure that integrates several tables within Excel to perform advanced analysis without using complex formulas.

Data Validation_Data Validation: is the tool that limits the types of data that can be entered into a cell.

DAX_Data Analysis Expressions: a formula language used in Power Pivot, Power BI and in data models to create advanced calculations.

Drill-Down_Detailed_Analysis: function to explore the details of a data summary, often in pivot tables or dashboards.

Dynamic Array_Matrix: an array that automatically updates when the source data changes. Functions such as UNIQUE or FILTER take advantage of dynamic arrays.

E

Excel Online: web version of Excel available through Microsoft 365, enabling real-time collaboration.

Excel Table_Table: a range of data formatted as a table to improve data organization and analysis.

External Data_Data: data imported into Excel from external sources such as SQL databases, CSV files, or online services.

External Link_External Link: a reference to a data item in a different Excel file.

F

Filter_Filter: a function to display only data that meets certain criteria.

Form Controls_Controls Form: interactive tools (e.g., check boxes, buttons) to create user interfaces directly in the worksheet.

Freeze Panes_Block Panes: function that keeps selected rows or columns visible while scrolling through the worksheet.

Function_Function: the default formula that performs specific calculations, such as SUM, CONCATENA or SEARCH.VERT.

G

Goal Seek_Research: the tool for finding an input value needed to achieve a deter- mined outcome.

Granularity_Granularity: level of detail in the data, particularly relevant in statistical analyses and pivot tables.

Gridlines_Grid: the lines that separate cells in the worksheet.

Group_Group: function that allows rows or columns to be grouped together for easy hiding or display.

H

Header Row_Row Header: the row at the top of a table that contains the column names.

Hyperlink_Hyperlink: a link to a document, Web site, or other location within the worksheet.

I

Icon Set_Set: conditional formatting function that uses icons to visually represent range-related values.

IF Function_Function IF: the logical function that returns one value if a condition is true and another if it is false.

Import_Import: process of transferring data from an external source into Excel.

Index_Index: the function that returns the value of a specific cell within a range.

L

Lookup_Research: the process of searching for a value in a range or table, e.g., functions such as SEARCH.VERT and SEARCH.ORIZZ.

M

Macro Recorder_Recorder of Macros: a tool that regi- strates a series of operations in Excel in order to reproduce them automatically in the future.

Macro: a series of automated commands recorded or written in VBA to perform repetitive operations.

Merge Cells_ Merge Cells: the function that combines two or more cells into a single cell.

Metadata_Metadata: descriptive information about a file, such as author, creation date, and file version.

N

Named Range_Interval: allows a cell range to be named for quick reference in formulas.

Nested Formula_Formula: a formula contained within another formula.

O

OFFSET_Move: function that returns a cell range shifted relative to a specified cell.

OneDrive: Microsoft's cloud storage service that allows synchronization of Excel files among multiple devices.

P

Pivot Table_Pivot Table: the tool for summarizing, analyzing, and exploring data dynamically.

Power Automate: automation tool that can interact with Excel to automate complex workflows.

Power Pivot: Add-on for handling large amounts of data and creating complex data models.

Power Query: the advanced function to import, transform and model data from different sources.

Protected View_Protected View: read-only mode to open files downloaded or received via email to reduce security risks.

Q

Quick Access Toolbar_Quick Access Toolbar: customizable toolbar for quick access to frequently used commands.

R

Range_Interval: a group of contiguous cells selected or used in a formula.

Refresh_Update: function used to refresh imported or linked data from external sources.

Relative Reference_Reference: a reference to a cell that fits when copied to another location.

Ribbon/Multifunctional Bar: Excel's top bar that organizes commands into tabs.

S

Slicer_Filter Data: the visual tool for filtering data in a table or pivot table.

Solver_Resolve: Add-on that finds the optimal solution to a problem based on specific constraints.

Spreadsheet(s): an Excel file that contains one or more sheets.

T

Table_Table: the tool for organizing data into rows and columns with advanced features such as filters and calculations.

Text to Columns_Text to Columns: a tool for dividing the contents of a cell into multiple columns based on delimiters such as commas or spaces.

Timeline_Timeline: visual filter in pivot tables that allows data to be filtered by time intervals.

Transpose_Transpose: the function that allows you to change rows to columns and vice versa.

V

Validation Rule_Rule: the criteria that control the data that can be entered into a cell.

VBA_Visual Basic for Applications: the programming language used to automate operations in Excel.

Vertical Lookup_CERCA.VERT: the function to look up a value in one column and return a corresponding result in another column.

W

Workbook_Workbook: an Excel file that can contain multiple worksheets.

Worksheet(s): a single page within an Excel workbook.

X

XML_Extensible Markup Language: structured file format used to import and export data into Excel.

Z

Zoom_Zoom: the tool to enlarge or reduce the view of a sheet.

BIBLIOGRAPHY

- Alexander M., Kusleika R., *Excel 2019 Power Programming with VBA* Wiley, Hoboken (NJ), 2018.
- Banfield C., Shakil M., *Excel 2016: Getting Results with VBA*, Apress, Berkeley (CA), 2016.
- Barbera M.L., Biasi M., *Advanced Excel: Handbook for data management, analysis and visualization*, Edizioni FAG, Rome,
- 2019. Basso F., *Excel for Business: Strategies for Managing, Analyzing and Presenting Data*, Franco Angeli, Milan, 2018.
- Benassi P., Saini S., *Excel data analysis*, Pearson, Milan, 2019.
- Bennett J.O., Briggs W.L.,*Using and Understanding Mathematics: A Quantitative Reasoning Approach*, Pearson, Boston (MA), 2018.
- Bianchini A., *Excel 2021 for everyone*, Hoepli, Milan, 2021.
- Bianchini A., *Practical Guide to Excel 2019*, Hoepli, Milan, Italy,
- 2019. Bill J., Juhasz S., *Excel 365 Formulas*, Holy Macro! Books, Uniontown (OH), 2022.
- Bini C., *Excel and VBA Finance and Data Analysis*, Apogeo, Milan, 2017.
- Carlberg C., *Business Analysis with Microsoft Excel*, Que Publishing, Indianapolis (IN), 2016.
- Dalgleish D., *Excel Pivot Table Recipes,* Apress, Berkeley (CA), 2007.
- Dixon H., *Excel for Project Management*, Independently Published, 2021.

- Fairhurst D.S., *Financial Modeling in Excel for Dummies*, Wiley, Hoboken (NJ), 2017.

- Foulkes L.,*Learn Microsoft Office 365: A Comprehensive Guide to Getting Started with Word, PowerPoint, Excel, Access, and Outlook*, Packt Publishing, Birmingham (UK), 2020.

- Franchini G., *Excel for business data analysis*, Franco Angeli, Milan, 2020.

- Goldmeier J., Duggirala P., *Dashboards for Excel*, Apress, Berkeley (CA), 2015.

- Gue E., *Excel Dashboards and Reports For Dummies*, Wiley, Hoboken (NJ), 2021.

- Harvey G., *Excel All-in-One For Dummies*, Wiley, Hoboken (NJ), 2021.

- Hermans F., *The Programmer's Guide to Excel*, Manning Publications, Shelter Island (NY), 2022.

- Jelen B., *Excel 2019 In Depth*, Que Publishing, Indianapolis (IN), 2018.

- Juhasz S., Juhász M., *Excel 2019 Pivot Tables and Introduction to Power Pivot*, Independently Published, 2019.

- Kyd C., *Excel Dashboard Reports*, Holy Macro! Books, Uniontown (OH), 2005.

- Mayes T.R., Shank T.M., *Financial Analysis with Microsoft Excel*, Cengage Learning, Boston (MA), 2018.

- Michaloudis J., Hong B., *101 Most Popular Excel Formulas*, Independently Published, 2018.

- Moretti A., *Excel for Business Intelligence*, LSWR Editions, Milan, Italy, 2021.

- Mount G., *Advancing into Analytics: From Excel to Python and R*, O'Reilly Media, Sebastopol (CA), 2021.
- Nelson S.L., *Excel Data Analysis For Dummies*, Wiley, Hoboken (NJ), 2014.
- Oz du Soleil, *Guerrilla Data Analysis Using Microsoft Excel*, Holy Macro! Books, Uniontown (OH), 2016.
- Patel Y., *Excel Power Query Beginner's Guide*, Packt Publishing, Birmingham (UK), 2020.
- Pisoni A., *Excel 2019: Complete Handbook for Beginners and Professionals*, FAG Editions, Rome, 2020.
- Pitch K., *Mastering Excel 2021: A Comprehensive Guide for Beginners*, Independently Published, 2021.
- Proctor M., *Beginning Excel VBA Programming*, Apress, Berkeley (CA), 2021.
- Puls K., Escobar M., *M is for (Data) Monkey: A Guide to the M Language in Excel Power Query*, Holy Macro! Books, Uniontown (OH), 2015.
- Syrstad T., Jelen B., *Excel VBA and Macros,* Que Publishing, Indianapolis (IN), 2015.
- Walkenbach J., *Excel 2019 Bible*, Wiley, Hoboken (NJ), 2018.
- Winston W.L., *Microsoft Excel Data Analysis and Business Modeling*, Microsoft Press, Redmond (WA), 2019.
- Zoccali R., *Excel VBA: Programming in Excel to work and improve performance*, Hoepli, Milan, 2020.

Made in the USA
Monee, IL
06 March 2025

13563889R00085